. . . Granting you peace and deliverance

Is my last gift to you.

This Book Belongs to:

It is a Gift from:

Goodbye, My Friend

CELEBRATING THE MEMORY OF A PET

DEVON O'DAY

Author of *My Angels Wear Fur*

SONGS BY KIM MCLEAN

RUTLEDGE HILL PRESS®

Nashville, Tennessee

A Division of Thomas Nelson Publishers

www.ThomasNelson.com

Published by Rutledge Hill Press, a division of Thomas Nelson, Inc., P.O. Box 141000, Nashville, Tennessee 37214.

Rutledge Hill Press books may be purchased in bulk for educational, business, fund-raising, or sales promotional use. For information, please e-mail SpecialMarkets@ThomasNelson.com.

ISBN-13: 978-1-4016-0313-7
ISBN-10: 1-4016-0313-0

Printed in China
06 07 08 09 10—5 4 3 2 1

Too many times,
        We miss the point.

It is in the simple love of a good friend,
        We find success, happiness, and joy.

We must always give thanks for

the furry angels that have blessed our lives,

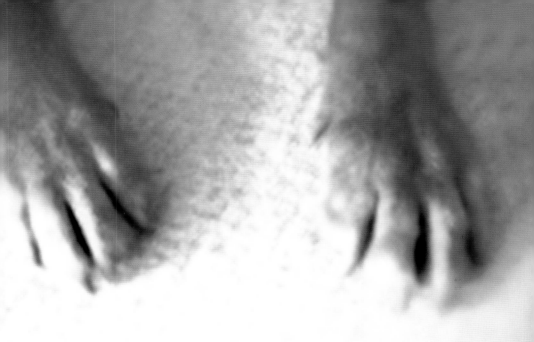

For it is through their

SACRIFICE

DEVOTION, *and* LOYALTY . . .

We learn to be better people.

Feel everything you must.
Let the pain be as big as it is.

Let the memories pour
like a summer rain and make rivers in your soul.
For as we return to those rivers,

Again

and again

and again,

We will begin to see the divine reason we were chosen.
We will realize how deeply we've been blessed.
It is in those rivers, we will learn the lessons our
humble teachers came to us to share.

This book is for all those
who have been greatly touched and left
forever changed by an animal angel.

How do I say goodbye to my best friend?

You've always been so faithful.

I've always needed so much.

You've never given less than your all.

I want to give you that back.

If money would buy you more time,

I'd gladly be a pauper to get

even a day more.

But that would be for me . . .

not you.

This is how I will remember you . . .

Sitting in the bay window,
begging to go out and chase the birds
from the feeders on the sill.

You thought me a sadist for saying no.

So close, and yet so far were those birds.

Yes,
this is how I will
remember you.

You never met a kid you didn't like, or a coyote you did.
Who'll sing bass when the train goes by?
Who'll make me feel safe when I go for walks at night?
I think I'm the only one who truly knows your bark
has always offered more to fear than your bite.

Unless of course, you were a *dog biscuit*
or a piece of *country ham*.

I'll miss you, Old Man.
I wish you pastures of goats
to tend till I get there.

They don't give you
a day off when you lose
A family member who
just happens to have fur.

I can't understand that.
I could have taken a day when my uncle died,
And I didn't even like him.
You were my precious angel.
You were my guardian.
You were my caretaker.

Doesn't the world know how much you meant to me?

I have always understood more than you realized.
I knew what the doctor said.
I knew why you cried.
I knew it was love that let me go.
I was a blessed creature.

To have come to this earth to be your pet
was a gift that I have only now begun to realize.
Your home was the best place I could have spent my earthly years.
Time with you was the best time I could have had.
You are just my favorite person . . . ever!

Oh, how lucky to have been me!

No matter how down I have ever felt,
  You knew just the thing to make me smile.

            It was a year to the day.
              A year . . . come and gone.

From the moment you left me,
It was springtime again.

And there in the place where
you now sleep forever,
A place where no flowers
have ever been planted,
Were two tulips sprung up
from the ground.

One for me, one for you.

A visitation I think.

We got her on the day we met.
She was the symbol of our love.

She was there when our children were born.
She was there when you lost your job,
And gave you purpose every day till you found one again.

She was there when we argued, and somehow
brought humor and the glue that healed us.

She was there when I couldn't dream anymore,
And reassured me until my dreams returned.

She was there when the kids had nightmares.
She was there when the storms raged.
She was there when we moved into the big house,
And there when we moved out.

On this day,
She is no longer with us.
And we will never be the same.

And the man climbed the hill
to the tree where he used to sit with her.

He carried her full weight up the steep hill.
He had to.
This is where he knew she needed to spend eternity.
It had to be him . . . *alone*.

No one could share this task.
It was his last kind act for a love so precious.
It was hard.
He struggled with every scoop of earth.

He lifted her body onto her favorite quilt.
He wrapped her gently, snugly, for sleep.
He surrounded her with dog biscuits,
her tennis balls, and her favorite toys.

Then he wept as he covered her forever.
He didn't care how loud he got.

He cried out so heaven would feel his pain.

He cried out so heaven would open its gates for her.

At the end of the ritual,
He sat near her as the sun set.
He was quiet.
He said goodbye and walked back down the hill,

Alone.

There is a place where the sunlight beams
hot and delicious on the cushions of the window seat.

I never realized there were cushions there, really . . .
until now.

Because you were always on those cushions,
Sprawled and soaking up the sun with guiltless pleasure.

It makes me smile to remember.

You would really love how the sun is shining today.
It's just the way you liked it.

Who knew such incredible friends
Would become of us?

Who knew saying goodbye would be so hard?

So how many times did you defend me?

How many times did you say,
"He's got every bit as much personality as a dog!"?

How many times did you stay in one position on the couch,
so as not to disturb my nap?

How many times did you make me purr?

Thank you.

I remember complaining about that early wake-up call.
You . . . with the leash in your mouth.
The world is always a little too cold at 6 a.m.

But you were insistent,
And I always went.

I woke up and walked today at 6 a.m., just for old time's sake.
I sure missed you.

Here at the water's edge, I sit watching the ducks swim
in peace because you are not here.
I know it made you smile today when I ran into
the water fully dressed and sent them flying loudly
in a million directions, just for you.

I sent them to the sky,
Where you can catch them now.

You will always
know when
the time is right
for goodbye.

It is a message sent
soul to soul.

On the last day,
I gave you everything you loved,
Everything the doctor said you couldn't have.

On the last day,
We drove with the windows open,
And you drank the wind you could no longer see.

On the last day,
I held you close to me and thanked you for being
The best friend one could ever have.

On the last day,
We made a perfect memory,
One that had to last forever.

Today I slipped on a pair of socks,
and one of the toes was completely
chewed away.

I thought of you.

I smiled.

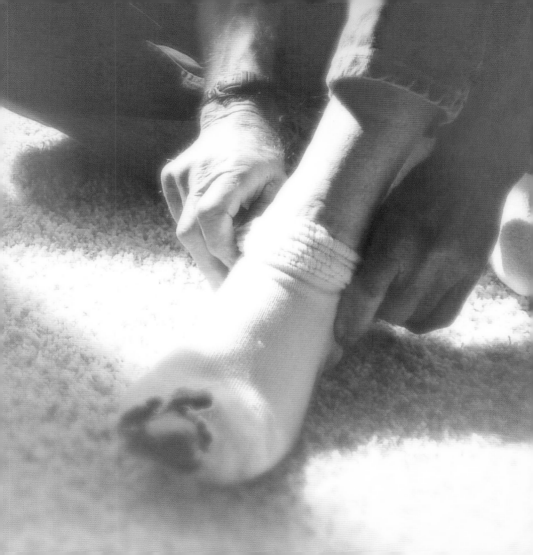

I wish only for an appreciation of life as you had.

Every day was a great big beautiful gulp of joy.

No matter what, life was glorious.

Thank you for making me see that glorious is always possible!

You always kept the loneliness away.

You always made me feel so safe and protected.

I guess you can do it even better now,

Since you have wings.

There is never a right way or a wrong way to grieve.

There is only the way you choose to experience it.

It is the hardest part of living.

It is beautiful in its truth.

It is over and lives on at the same time.

I want to imagine that the people I have loved,
That have passed over . . .

Are caring for the animals I have loved,
That have passed over . . .

And that they'll all be waiting for me,
When I, too, cross that bridge.

The smell of your mane
as I buried my face in it.

You always smelled real and organic.

The scent lingers in my memory

And in my heart.

So as I look at the dream catcher woven from your mane,

Swinging in the breeze in the window above my bed,

I know that you are running on that wind,

Through my dreams

The thunder in my heart,

The road for us will never end, my friend.

The wind chimes on the
front porch catch
the breeze and
I wonder if
it's you.

I prayed for a *miracle.*

I prayed for *answers.*

I prayed for *peace.*

You must have prayed for *me.*

I galloped over the moon this time,
       Yes, I galloped over the moon.
With the angel herd waiting,
       The wind calling my name,
There were wings on my hooves,

           And oh, how I flew.

I was the echo across the Grand Canyon,
       The echo you heard,
My hoofbeats like heartbeats,

           I chased the sky.

And with the freedom you gave me,
   I caught it this time.

     I caught it this time.

       I caught it this time.

I will wait for you . . .
Here where the air is clear and cool.

I will wait for you . . .
Here where the angels know my name.

I will wait for you . . .
Here where I can always see you.

I will wait for you . . .
Here where the rainbow ends.

You wouldn't believe how much fun this place is!!!

There is *always* a chew toy.

There are *always* a bunch of kids to play with.

There is *always* a fireplace waiting after a full day of play.

I hear your tears.

If only you knew where your heart has allowed me to go,

You would never cry again.

It is in
the small things
that we learn the
biggest lessons

Will you Chase bees in heaven?

Will you bark at the gardeners?

Will you be as persnickety about your bed?

Will you beg for salmon and rice the way I made it for you?

Will you be watching over me, like you've always done?

I just wondered. . .

Will you be waiting for me?

Dear Angels,
Take care of my best friend.
He doesn't like to sleep alone.
He hates loud noises.

He loves spaghetti.

I remember the day you came home with me.

You had me from 'meow'.

Those blue eyes . . .

That insistent purr . . .

The way you got in my suitcase when I was packing for a trip . . .

You demanded me.

I have never had anyone want me that much.

And . . .

I never will again.

When you watch the night sky,

it is amazing that you can

find a collection of stars that

look like someone you love

if you connect the dots.

Comfort is
born out of
Legacy.

Goodbye, My Friend

Goodbye, My Friend is a gift book of consolation, peace, and comfort for those who are losing or have lost a dear pet. It is a book with original music to allow grief and healing for the loss of a beloved family member who just happens to be a pet.

Both the book and accompanying CD have been created to be experienced simultaneously, to bring peace and hope. Currently in the United States, more people have pets than have children. People care deeply for their animal family members. Pet grief is a rising need in the hearts of animal lovers worldwide.

This book was written by Devon O'Day, author of *My Angels Wear Fur*. The original music is by Kim McLean, an award-winning singer/songwriter/recording artist.

It is for all those who have been greatly touched and left forever changed by an animal angel.

The Author's Free Gift to You

Publish and celebrate a lifetime of pet memories through My Pet Story™. Showcase the stories, photos, special accomplishments and other mementos that defined your pet's personality through our entry level product. Once created, share your pet's story with friends and family online via our Web site **www.mypetstory.com**. Print your pet's story, e-mail it to loved ones, and access your account as often as you'd like to modify text or pictures on your site.

My Pet Story makes it easy to share meaningful memories. Our simple online steps take you through the process. Just access the Web link listed below and type in the promotional code to get started.

Promotional Site: www.MyPetStory.com/GoodbyeMyFriend

Promotional Code: MeM4Pets